Contents

Using this book   2

Practising spelling at home   3

Spellings sets 1–40   4–43

Word list for Years 3 and 4   44

Word list for Years 5 and 6   45

My spelling targets   46–47

My tricky spellings   48

Using this book

This book will help you to record and practise new spellings using the strategy, 'Look, Say, Cover, Write, Check'. Perfect for weekly spelling practice, the book contains space for 40 sets of 15 spellings. After each set of spellings, a short writing activity encourages you to practise using spellings in context.

How to use this book

Before you begin, carefully remove the bookmark from the inside back cover.

When you are given a new set of spellings to learn, write the spelling rule in the space provided. Then copy the spellings neatly into the first column of the table.

Look at the first word. Are there any tricky bits or any spelling patterns?

Say the word. How many syllables are there? What sounds can you hear?

Cover up the word using the bookmark. Then write the word in the second column, remembering what it looks and sounds like.

Check to see if you spelt the word correctly. If you did, put a tick next to it. If you made any mistakes, cover the first column and try writing the word again in the third column.

Spellings set 1 The suffix -ly   **Date** 14th October 2019

Look, say and cover	Write and check	Write and check
completely	completly	completely ✓
finally	finally ✓	finally ✓

Word lists (pages 44–45)
Handy copies of spellings you need to know in Years 3, 4, 5 and 6 are included.

My spelling targets (pages 46–47)
Teachers can record your spelling targets and achievements on these pages.

My tricky spellings (page 48)
Use this page to make a note of any tricky spellings requiring more practice.

Practising spelling at home

Confidence in spelling helps children to write more freely and more imaginatively. Children become more confident in spelling by practising over and over again, and this is best done in fun and interesting ways. Make short bursts of spelling practice part of children's daily routine.

Top tips

Use Scrabble® pieces to practise spellings. Mix up the letters of words from the child's spelling list. Read one word at a time and ask the child to find the correct letters and place them on the board in the correct order.

Create your own word searches using words from the child's spelling list. Ask the child to colour in or highlight the words in different colours as they find them.

Ask the child to write words from their spelling list in bubble writing. Encourage them to decorate each letter with a different colour or pattern. Display the child's bubble writing creations somewhere they will be seen each day.

Ask the child to write a short story using all the words in their spelling list. Ask them to underline or highlight the spelling words in the story.

Ask the child to write a 'silly sentence' for each of the words in their spelling list. For example, for the word 'fruit' they could write the sentence, 'Aliens love eating bright pink smelly fruit'.

Play a memory game. Create two identical sets of word cards with words from the child's spelling list. Shuffle the cards and place them face down on a table. Take it in turns to turn over two cards at a time. Who can find the most pairs?

Write down the words in the child's spelling list inside other letters. For example, abhaeearthskue contains the word 'earth'. Ask the child to circle the hidden words using coloured pens. How many words can they find in one minute?

Write the words in the child's spelling list out on a piece of paper with the letters scrambled up. Ask the child to unscramble the letters and write the words correctly next to the scrambled words.

Together, make up mnemonics for spellings children find particularly difficult. For example, Brainy Elephants Can Add Up Sums Easily for 'because'.

Spellings set 1   Date

Look, say and cover	Write and check	Write and check

Write a **question** using one of the words.

Spellings set 2   Date

Look, say and cover	Write and check	Write and check

Write a **statement** using one of the words.

Spellings set 3

Date

Look, say and cover	Write and check	Write and check

Write a **command** using one of the words.

Schofield & Sims ● My spelling book

Spellings set 4

Date

Look, say and cover	Write and check	Write and check

Write an **exclamation** using one of the words.

Spellings set 5　　　　　　　　　　　　　Date

Look, say and cover	Write and check	Write and check

Write a **question** using one of the words.

Spellings set 6 　　　　　　　　　　　　　　　　　　Date

Look, say and cover	Write and check	Write and check

Write a **statement** using one of the words.

Schofield & Sims • My spelling book

Spellings set 7   Date

Look, say and cover	Write and check	Write and check

Write a **command** using one of the words.

Spellings set 8

Date

Look, say and cover	Write and check	Write and check

Write an **exclamation** using one of the words.

Spellings set 9   Date

Look, say and cover	Write and check	Write and check

Write a **question** using one of the words.

Spellings set 10   Date

Look, say and cover	Write and check	Write and check

Write a **statement** using one of the words.

_____

Spellings set 11   Date

Look, say and cover	Write and check	Write and check

Write a **command** using one of the words.

Spellings set 12   Date

Look, say and cover	Write and check	Write and check

Write an **exclamation** using one of the words.

___

Spellings set 13

Date

Look, say and cover	Write and check	Write and check

Write a **question** using one of the words.

Spellings set 14

Date

Look, say and cover	Write and check	Write and check

Write a **statement** using one of the words.

Spellings set 15

Date

Look, say and cover	Write and check	Write and check

Write a **command** using one of the words.

Spellings set 16 _____ Date _____

Look, say and cover	Write and check	Write and check

Write an **exclamation** using one of the words.

_____

Spellings set 17   Date

Look, say and cover	Write and check	Write and check

Write a **question** using one of the words.

Spellings set 18

Date

Look, say and cover	Write and check	Write and check

Write a **statement** using one of the words.

Spellings set 19   Date

Look, say and cover	Write and check	Write and check

Write a **command** using one of the words.

Spellings set 20

Date

Look, say and cover	Write and check	Write and check

Write an **exclamation** using one of the words.

Schofield & Sims ● **My spelling book**

Spellings set 21

Date

Look, say and cover	Write and check	Write and check

Write a **question** using one of the words.

Spellings set 22   Date

Look, say and cover	Write and check	Write and check

Write a **statement** using one of the words.

Spellings set 23

Date

Look, say and cover	Write and check	Write and check

Write a **command** using one of the words.

Spellings set 24   Date

Look, say and cover	Write and check	Write and check

Write an **exclamation** using one of the words.

Spellings set 25 Date

Look, say and cover	Write and check	Write and check

Write a **question** using one of the words.

Spellings set 26   Date

Look, say and cover	Write and check	Write and check

Write a **statement** using one of the words.

Spellings set 27   Date

Look, say and cover	Write and check	Write and check

Write a **command** using one of the words.

Spellings set 28

Date

Look, say and cover	Write and check	Write and check

Write an **exclamation** using one of the words.

Spellings set 29   Date

Look, say and cover	Write and check	Write and check

Write a **question** using one of the words.

Spellings set 30

Date

Look, say and cover	Write and check	Write and check

Write a **statement** using one of the words.

Spellings set 31

Date

Look, say and cover	Write and check	Write and check

Write a **command** using one of the words.

Spellings set 32   Date

Look, say and cover	Write and check	Write and check

Write an **exclamation** using one of the words.

_____

Spellings set 33   Date

Look, say and cover	Write and check	Write and check

Write a **question** using one of the words.

Spellings set 34   Date

Look, say and cover	Write and check	Write and check

Write a **statement** using one of the words.

Spellings set 35   Date

Look, say and cover	Write and check	Write and check

Write a **command** using one of the words.

Spellings set 36   Date

Look, say and cover	Write and check	Write and check

Write an **exclamation** using one of the words.

Spellings set 37

Date

Look, say and cover	Write and check	Write and check

Write a **question** using one of the words.

Spellings set 38

Date

Look, say and cover	Write and check	Write and check

Write a **statement** using one of the words.

Spellings set 39   Date

Look, say and cover	Write and check	Write and check

Write a **command** using one of the words.

42   Schofield & Sims ● **My spelling book**

Spellings set 40

Date

Look, say and cover	Write and check	Write and check

Write an **exclamation** using one of the words.

Word list for Years 3 and 4

accident(ally)
actual(ly)
address
answer
appear
arrive
believe
bicycle
breath
breathe
build
busy/business
calendar
caught
centre
century
certain
circle
complete
consider
continue
decide
describe
different
difficult
disappear
early
earth
eight/eighth
enough
exercise
experience
experiment

extreme
famous
favourite
February
forward(s)
fruit
grammar
group
guard
guide
heard
heart
height
history
imagine
important
increase
interest
island
knowledge
learn
length
library
material
medicine
mention
minute
natural
naughty
notice
occasion(ally)
often
opposite

ordinary
particular
peculiar
perhaps
popular
position
possess(ion)
possible
potatoes
pressure
probably
promise
purpose
quarter
question
regular
reign
remember
sentence
separate
special
straight
strange
strength
suppose
therefore
though/although
thought
through
various
weight
woman/women

Word list for Years 5 and 6

accommodate
accompany
according
achieve
aggressive
amateur
ancient
apparent
appreciate
attached
available
average
awkward
bargain
bruise
category
cemetery
committee
communicate
community
competition
conscience
conscious
controversy
convenience
correspond
criticise (critic + ise)
curiosity
definite
desperate
determined
develop
dictionary
disastrous

embarrass
environment
equip (-ped, -ment)
especially
exaggerate
excellent
existence
explanation
familiar
foreign
forty
frequently
government
guarantee
harass
hindrance
identity
immediate(ly)
individual
interfere
interrupt
language
leisure
lightning
marvellous
mischievous
muscle
necessary
neighbour
nuisance
occupy
occur
opportunity
parliament

persuade
physical
prejudice
privilege
profession
programme
pronunciation
queue
recognise
recommend
relevant
restaurant
rhyme
rhythm
sacrifice
secretary
shoulder
signature
sincere(ly)
soldier
stomach
sufficient
suggest
symbol
system
temperature
thorough
twelfth
variety
vegetable
vehicle
yacht

My spelling targets

Date set	Target	Adult's comments	Date met

Date set	Target	Adult's comments	Date met

My tricky spellings